The Lunar Lan

By

Paul Gerard McDermott

Father Son Holy Ghost
Same place same time the story goes
Not before nor since has seen this apparition
Other than at Christ's baptism
The most important moment
In the history of man
Unless your hopes are pinned on
The lunar landing

In the great mausoleum
Is a portrait of a woman
With a priceless smile
She has love on her mind
Which is the attraction
And though her legacy lives on
Her mystery's as unfathomable
As the mind that made conceivable
A vision so divine
In blatant mortal terms
As if it were the gospel
According to Leonardo

Love unkissed forever lives
And with everything is blessed
Out of solitude till death
Is the poet's alms
Love kissed leads a double life
And with everything is halved
Out of companionship that dies
In another's arms

I love him
In equal measure
As an inch
2 . 5 centimetres
I can't explain
No more
Than a fish can
The water
The pain
My heart endures
Other than
It's giving birth
To the same
Mortal power
As divine
As God

Marriage is a church
An institution of truth
Truth is a vessel
Containing love
Drink of the vessel
And uphold truth
Fill the vessel
And establish love
Where truth is upheld
Love is established
It's not bricks and mortar
But flesh and blood

Family is a temple
A place of worship
On hallowed ground
Take the shoes off
In the presence of love
Validate existence
Who from its father
Is added to its children
In the generation gap
Come barefoot to the truth
Diamonds in the mud
Are missed by big boots

A rule for man
As tested in the crucible
By the skirts of its raiment
The intangible is tangible
Nothing exists
If existence is futile
But the universe is evidence
That nothing is impossible
A footprint on the moon
A handprint in a cave
Is it what is believed
Or what is conveyed
Science explains the least of things
Religion bows to the endless
But faith to move mountains
Is void without love

Echoes of man
Ripple on earth
In space and time
People are words
To the great song
That sing the gods
Whose instruments
Silently pluck
Living beings
Of flesh and blood
Out of the womb
For want and worth
To grace the stones
On which they walk
And raise with hands
In noble cause
Acknowledgement
Such tools are blessed
With divine works
And mortal tasks

From stepping stone
To stepping stone
All are islands
Together alone
Historic steps
Tread and tread
One to another
Avoiding death

To the theologian's
Bewilderment
For the philosopher's
Employment
At the intellectual's
Expense
In the teacher's
Lesson
The child asked
Who is God

Does one belief
Negate another
Or are two truths
Multiples of one

Does every faith
Come to the same conclusion
Can every way
Go in the same direction
Cos every grace
Is of the same salvation

The poetry premiers the idea
The words furnish the product

When she with love
Holds he with truth
He with truth
Holds she with love

She was the Sun
To his Earth
She was the poet
To his words
She was the beat
To his heart
She was the paint
To his brush
She was the soul
To his flesh
She was the opus
To his work
She was the truth
To his love
She was the face
To his God

In the far reaches of the universe
Is the chance encounter calculator
That delivers every birth and death
To the last digit of Pi
From the first recorded Sine
Pythagoras knew it well
As the sum of X + Y
Every woman every man
Is a product of its time

No opinion
On the matter
To the problem
Was the closer
Interfacing
The dilemma
With a modem
And computer

The beautiful thoughts
Escape me
Just ugly words
Encase me
In a cage wrought
Inside me
Where Paradise lost
Finds me
In forbidden love
Tempting me
From obedience to God
Condemning me
To a life of lust
Injuring me
With my own sword
Piercing me
In a broken heart
Sentencing me
To a concrete box

I cannot see
I cannot hear
I cannot feel
The bubble
That keeps me
From the world
That keeps the world
From me
Everyone's got one
Together alone
But God help us
If it bursts

What has always been
In the heart and mind
Of what will always be
Is the spirit of man

Beauty unfabricated
Youth uncorrupted
Love unadulterated
Truth unvarnished

Beauty youth love truth
Are different fountains
Of the same happiness
Body soul heart mind
Are different satisfactions
Of the same thirst

On a slow boat
Did sail my soul
He on the helm
Me on the sail
When came a storm
I feared a ghost
Was in the wind
To test my will
When came a calm
I feared a voice
Was in the still
To steal my joy
But when we sailed
I knew my world
Was in safe hands
To reach my goal

A walk on part in the universe
A lead role in a concrete box
If the world's a stage
And life is the play
Then man's a puppet
With no strings attached
Is this recognised
As free will of choice
The former mystery
The latter destiny

My testimony
Life put a hurt on me
My epitaph
I put a hurt on life

The kaleidoscope world
Is of a law universal
That manipulates and controls
The plastic particles
That pattern the spy hole
Of the vision's ideal
That is infinitely possible
Through the eye of a needle

I looked who'd been a lonely child
In the window to the soul
And a stigma on the pupil
Had learned to colour the world
With the thorn and not the rose
Of a love that did not grow
Like a cancer does not know
That it is killing its host

It was the handmaiden said
That she was just average
And the prince who met his match
In common courtesy said
Just average hopes are met
On the road to happiness

A minor miracle
Not inexplicable
Coincidental
A happened on remedy
As resulted seemingly
From asking in prayer
In itself a crooked answer
That knows the need
But when the prayer stops
So do the coincidences
Not especially to prove
More exclusively to choose
Faith over doubt
To hear the discerning voice
That is master of who you are
In the ears to your heart

The many routes
That lead to truth
The origin of which
Is living proof
The unexplained
Reason for life
As evident
In the search for love
The purpose of which
Is obvious
Can't be defined
In a concrete box

Make such an end
As is worthy of a song
And the next life will begin
On wings if at all

Could the first naked ape
Who made a handprint in a cave
In recognition of himself
In the scheme of things
Acknowledging
The greater power of creation
Be the first man much like Adam
Having plucked a poisoned fruit
With the power to envisage
Life death and universe
Inadvertently stumbling
By chance or design
On the immortal soul
And learning of its love so possessed
Humanity as set apart
From the beasts of the field

A vessel of love
A chalice of blood
A breaking of bread
A building of church
A marriage if faith
A children of truth
A planet of Earth
An answer of yes

Temples of the world
Places of worship
Marriage family
Communion tablets
Human endeavour
Inventing the future
The science of facts
The world was flat
Not with a whimper
But with a bang
The bubble bursts
This primal planet
Like taking a pin
To civilization
The altar consecrated
To a world with cracks

Natural selection
Selfish gene
Mortal coil
Primal scream
Eternal progress
Perpetual change
Collective conscious
Universal womb
Divine nature
Holy Communion
Existence measures
Human condition

It's a fortunate soul
That sees the shadow
It casts on the world
For the visible source
Is the light that shines
On the object of its love

Fear of death
Born of survival
Reaches for love
To be eternal
If love can't be had
Life is futile
And nothing exists
To save the world
The known universe
Is a certain truth
Something exists
And man is proof
Love is everything
That gives credence
To the matter of being
Science and religion

Science and religion
Are like feuding twins
Dogma dogs invention
Technology nips at Heaven

If the hands of man
Are the greatest tools
In all creation
Surely the designer
That engineered them
Was installed with equipment
Of a greater architecture

Hidden in a hollow hill
The foetus primal
Incubation of civilization
Not yet born of its womb
Dreams of many pillared halls
On the brink of reason
Whose purpose belief
At the door of evolution's
Printed hand of destiny
Is loves epiphany
Chosen to represent
The bigger picture
Of creation's architecture
Before power over everything
Gives it fire
To fight fear in the night
That falls victim to the predator
As a scream pierces
Its trembling heart
Hears a ghostly stealth drag another off

Death is greater than us
None can argue with that
But life is greater than death
In which we take comfort
With the sole purpose
Of being the stimulus
For the greater good
Most can agree as such

A right to life
All men possess
In love will land
Or be lost in space
In truth will meet
On even terms
The day that sees more
Than mortality allows

The great bird
That fills the universe
Man captured
The first step
To eternal reward
In moon dust
Trembling heart
Of a captive bird
Free the soul
Brave new world's
Chariot of the gods
Here and now

The moment passed
Too late made a start
Too soon had quit
Just now caught up

Youth and beauty
Build the future
Truth and love
The bricks and mortar
Here and now
The sacred altar
There and then
The occupier

Wants to believe
Already does
Could be a slave
Already is

Something
Time can't keep
Somewhere
Space can't reach
Somehow
Does can't heed
Someone
Is can't be

The pursuit of happiness
Is a contradiction in terms
The happy pursuit
Is a motivation that yearns
It's not the pilgrimage
But the pilgrim
That takes on the image
Of the betterment
A veneer facade
Is not solid wood
Solid space remarked
Inventing the truth
Love exists
To move the soul
Towards what is good
Like gravity pulls
Having been like this
In the place before birth
Becoming like this
Is happiness

Beauty in body
Tender my kiss
Truth in mind
Answer me yes
Love in heart
Render me blessed
Youth in soul
Ever I live

The cave dwellers
A race apart
From other beasts
Of the earth
Had minds of thought
That held beliefs
Of other worlds
Beyond the veil
Of instinct
Did procreate
And survive
Like insect life
Of feelings
Did have a heart
And nurture love
Like animals
Of spirit
Were set apart
From all other
To know the good
Where life was found
Did celebrate
Where life was lost
Did venerate
To pay homage
To flesh and blood
For birth and death
To be continued

Enter the universe
In the same naked truth
Exit the universe
In unique clothes of love

If for all the good you do
All the bad in the world
Is not undone
Do good anyway
If for all the love you feel
All the hate in the world
Is not touched
Feel love anyway
If for all the truth you adhere to
All the lies in the world
Adhere not
Adhere to truth anyway
If for all the people you value
All the people of the world
Value not
Value people anyway

The glitter of the stars
Leads the children of the earth
Down the garden path
To reflect Paradise lost
Finds the face looking back
The face Narcissus loved
And the voice of Echo's heart
The eternal reward

It grieves the soul
To soil the hands
Which aches the heart
That twists the mind
To hate the world
And curse all men
Till can't stomach
Its own poison

The Devil's minions
Are quick to point out
Who goes to Heaven
And who goes to Hell
A guilty plea
A way out of Hell
Protect the innocent
A way into Heaven

The wolf in a fleece
The flock that it leads
The woolly head sheep
The lost they will be
The innocent souls
The life it will steal
The danger is real
The greener the field

Destroy all monsters
Devilish minions
Blood sucking vampires
Soulless Frankensteins
Hell bent necromancers
Wolves of mortal sin
Ghosts of witches past
Demons of the mind
Power mad scientists
Invading aliens
Zombie apocalypses
Abominations

The measure of a man
Is in his warrior
In the battle for truth
Fighting love's corner
For the salt of the earth
To cry out its nature
The sword that slays
And the sword that saves
Were forged
In the same fire

What is brought to the table
Of human endeavour
Could not fill a thimble
Of divine measure

Random acts of love
For the indiscriminate
Feeds the ducks
In the park
Certain words of truth
For the village idiot
Reads a book
On the facts

Since no intellect
Can penetrate
And no language
Can explain
The universe
And its nature
Human thought
Is guided
To contemplate
The divine
This Earth
Perfect in design
It seems impossible
A single mind
Did not create it
That there is no plan

Fresh mother
Breasts full
Of ambrosia
For the world
Holds the future
By the hand
With faith no more
Than humankind

Love that asks
Is always answered
Truth that tells
Is always questioned

Progress
A good word
Means going forward
Said Moses
Yes
A good word
Means affirmative
Said Jesus
Love
A good word
Means devoted
Said God
Plucked
A good word
Means selected
Said the snake

When madness dogs the heels
Of genius
Pay no heed
But to Van Gough
When poison judges
New ideals
Drink and live
Like Socrates
When freedom peacefully
beats empires
Fight the fight
Gandhi fought
When life is cheap
Among the great
Tears will flow
Jesus wept

On the edge
Was afraid that love
Would drive him mad
Made his bed
Was afraid that truth
Would catch him up
Loved is life
Was afraid that flesh
Would spill his blood
Met with death
Was afraid that breath
Would leave him sad

The spirit is a power
Added to the body
Because alone
The body cannot endure
The spirit desires
To remain with the body
Because without
It knows nothing of this world

The pain of this world
Is a blessing in the next
It serves the soul
To break the heart

In the body
Is an instrument
Of torture
In the mind
Is a cruel
Gaoler
In the heart
Is a dungeon
Of despair
In the soul
Is a freedom
That delivers

Many lived and died
By the sword and by the shield
The sword pierced their hearts
The shield saved their souls
Battles were won and lost
Victory was never sure
The war ravished the earth
Heaven was the cause

Printed in Great
Britain
by Amazon

31480126R00018